Preparing for your OKR program

BASTIN GERALD

WITH SENTHIL RAJAGOPALAN

9 781365 528361

Table of
Contents

01 Why OKRs?   1

02 How are businesses   17
    optimizing their
    execution?

03 What is iterative   27
    business execution?

04 What are OKRs?   35

05 We frequently review   49
    employee performance.
    Aren't we already
    iterating faster?

06 What does success look   59
    like?

07 How can you adopt   67
    OKRs successfully?

08 Why should start-ups   75
    embrace OKRs?

09 How can OKRs help   83
    remote performance?

10 Are OKR tools better   91
    than OKRs with
    spreadsheets?

11 How does the OKR   97
    framework compare
    to the Balanced
    Scorecard?

Introduction

You don't have to be great to start, but you have to start to be great.

 **Zig Ziglar**

Celebrated businessman and motivational speaker Zig Ziglar shared the above quote to help listeners realize that expecting perfection from yourself and your team right off the bat isn't realistic. Instead, practice and experience can add up to greatness over time. When it comes to OKRs, or Objectives and Key Results, this could not be more accurate.

OKRs have become the goal management and execution framework preferred by leaders and disruptors in the tech industry. Today we are seeing widespread adoption of OKRs outside the tech industry; commercial banks, insurance companies, Wall Street firms, automotive companies, energy companies, educational institutions, consumer goods, healthcare organizations and even progressive government agencies are all adopting OKRs.

That being said, it won't help to roll out the OKR framework without well-thought out preparations in place. If you're reading this book, you know this already. This book will give you a comprehensive background of OKRs that can help you not only understand the mechanics of the methodology, but also the culture you must institute in your company as a leader, and what makes OKRs your best option for executing your strategy.

This book will help you lay a strong foundation for your OKR program so that when it comes time to launch the framework in your business, you'll have all the tools you need to succeed.

1

Why OKRs?

Why do you need OKRs?

Why do I need to adopt OKRs?

This is the most common question consultants hear from businesses. Typically, the individuals asking this question are either new to OKRs, or have no background information on the subject.

To an untrained eye, the OKR framework may look like another employee performance management system. And for individuals that already get all their KPI information from their company dashboards or business intelligence solutions, they might not feel they need a new method.

Why do we need to invest our time in a new methodology? And on top of that, potentially invest in a new software tool?

"Why do we need to invest our time in a new methodology? And on top of that, potentially invest in a new software tool?" The response to these questions is short and simple— most of the time, you don't know what you don't know. Unless you are able to get a clear picture of what's working and what isn't, how do you know what to improve, remove, or add in your company processes?

10 advantages for businesses that use OKRs

Many individuals in business have seen the introduction, the proliferation, and the adoption of new technologies and processes.

In manufacturing, they once had line manufacturing, which progressed to cellular manufacturing. In the field of project management, teams have rapidly shifted from the

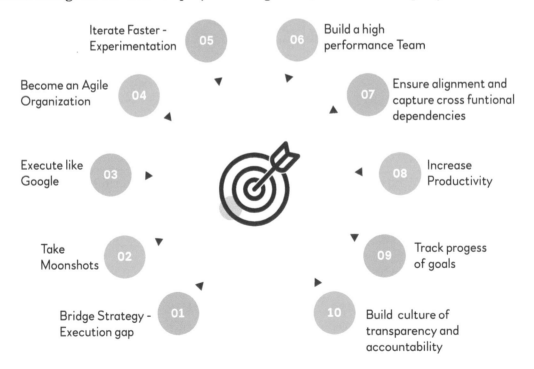

Figure 1.1: Ten advantages of businesses that plan and manage OKRs correctly

traditional waterfall methodology to the new and improved agile methodology.

Similarly, a change is already happening in the broader business world; now, it's the age of iterative business execution. That's one of the many advantages of OKRs; they enable you to execute your business strategies and get them done faster— iteratively. Companies that properly plan out and manage their OKRs can achieve a number of things that they previously never thought possible with their size and resources (Fig. 1.1).

1. Bridge Strategy- Execution Gap: A number of studies, including ones from the Harvard Business Review, have shown that approximately 70% of strategies fail due to poor execution. OKRs are a great goal management and execution framework for companies that would like to bridge the Strategy-Execution gap.

2. Take Moonshots: In 1962, President John F. Kennedy gave a speech at Rice University where he declared: "We choose to go to the moon in this decade". JFK did not set that goal by knowing how this goal could be achieved or by assuring everyone it would be easy. This ambitious vision energized an entire country to rally behind the cause, setting in motion a series of plans and achievements that resulted in accomplishing what once was considered "impossible"— "sending man to the moon". More recently, successful technology companies have been taking "Moonshots" achieving "seemingly impossible goals" using OKRs as their execution framework.

3. Execute Like Google: Google has a long list of achievements other than being the world's most successful search engine: Adsense, Gmail, Youtube, Android, Chrome, Google Maps and Google Docs. Google started using OKRs when they were a 40-person startup and continue to use them today, even as they have 140,000+ employees. They have repeatedly credited OKRs as one of the top reasons for their successful execution. For companies in every industry, "To execute like Google" is a dream and a great reason to adopt OKRs.

4. Build an Agile Organization: A Mckinsey study based on the S&P 500 Index found that the average life-span of large companies fell from 61 years in 1958 to about 18 years in 2011. Today businesses operate in a VUCA market (volatile, uncertain, complex, ambiguous) where market demands change frequently. Startups rapidly develop innovations, making it difficult for traditional organizations to keep up with their pace. So building an agile organization that can rapidly respond to market demands is key to thriving today. OKRs are an ideal framework to build an agile organization.

5. Iterate Faster: Booking.com reportedly runs more than 1,000 rigorous tests simultaneously with a total of more than 25,000 tests a year, according to Harvard Business School Professor, Stefan Thomke. Booking.com runs quadrillions (millions of billions) of landing-page permutations at any given time. This culture of experimentation has helped "transform the company from a small Dutch start-up to the world's largest online accommodation platform in less than two decades". OKRs provide a great framework to nurture this culture of experimentation and help companies to iterate faster and win in the marketplace.

6. Build a High Performance Team: Smart investors in start-ups often value the quality of the founding team more than the idea itself. With availability of capital ceasing to be a problem for most qualified companies, having a high performance team can be the ultimate differentiator. OKRs improve Employee Engagement and can be a great tool to build high performance teams for startups and enterprises alike.

7. Ensure Alignment: As companies grow, the gaps between corporate and various business units can grow too, resulting in these units executing in silos. OKRs by definition encourage departments and teams to align and contribute to company goals and other departments' goals. Alignment happens when there is a shared vision and in-depth understanding of each other's goals. This enables teams to execute with focus and compliment each other's efforts.

8. Increase Productivity: Multi-tasking is the number one enemy of productivity. With the number of distractions multiplying for employees, OKRs can enable "deep work" and improve productivity. OKRs bring in "Focus" for teams and individuals at every level, and encourage users to only work on 3-5 OKRs at any given time. This can increase productivity across the board.

9. Track Progress of Goals: With OKRs, goals are broken down into interim milestones which are tracked through regular weekly check-ins. Check-ins, along with regular review meetings, are one of the top reasons that companies achieve their goals.

10. Build a culture of Transparency and Accountability: The OKR framework is great for building a culture of transparency and accountability. Company-level OKRs are visible for everyone, and so are the OKRs for most departments. Departments like M&A (Mergers & Acquisitions) that need to maintain confidentiality due to legal reasons may be the exception. Transparency empowers people as they are able to view the goals and progress reports for all of their coworkers and can see how their work is connected to the rest of the company. Alignment of OKRs clearly establishes ownership for execution and helps build a culture of accountability.

The Benefits of OKRs

The OKR framework helps solve some of the most common challenges that companies of all sizes and in all industries face. OKRs can help resolve issues with focus, alignment, commitment, measurement, and even complacency.

Often, companies are not proactive but rather reactive to these types of challenges. Business

Figure 1.2: *Five problem areas for businesses. All of these can be improved using OKRs.*

leaders can be slow to realize where the issues in their company are rooted, and identifying these company issues late wastes time and resources.

Challenges with Focus

If you're anything like the majority of business leaders, chances are you always want to accomplish a lot more than what you are currently doing, and usually in a shorter period. Your team has endless priorities: from new projects to new campaigns, new hires, new training

programs, conflict resolution, and stakeholder management. Sometimes it feels like the list never ends. When everything is a priority, and everything is urgent, your team will struggle to choose where to focus their energy.

Which tasks need to be started first? Which tasks are high-priority? What's the project that will have the highest impact? Which customers' needs should you address first?

If you do not put the first things first, then the next few things may not matter.

It's essential to prioritize everything from a business standpoint. What are the 3 to 5 things that you want to achieve for the rest of this year? How are you going to meet those objectives on a quarter by quarter basis?

It is crucial to pick your battles. When priorities are clear, the path to achieving those becomes clear. That prioritization must take the mission, vision, and strategy of your business into account. When business leaders set their priorities at the top level of the organization, it will

FOCUS

If you chase two rabbits, both will escape

enable teams at lower levels to select their own projects according to the company's priorities, and get the company moving in the same direction. When the paths are clear, you can propel forward more effectively, and you and your team reach your destination faster.

Challenges with Alignment

Organizations of all sizes— from start-ups to SMBs to large, multinational enterprises— all

struggle with the issue of focus. However, there is a bigger problem between teams, departments, branches, and that is the lack of overall company alignment.

A CEO might have clear targets set from her and the board's perspective. However, if the executives and managers next in the hierarchy do not focus on the same priorities, then there is a good chance that the company will not achieve its objectives. If the directors and VPs have a different vision than the front-line employees, that indicates that the department is not as effective or productive as it could be.

The issue of alignment applies across departments as well. If the marketing department's Q1 OKRs are set without regard for the sales or the engineering department's OKRs, it's a recipe for a disastrous upcoming quarter.

When it comes to company-wide alignment, your goal should always be 100%.

Every employee in your company has daily tasks and projects that contribute to the business's success. But do you know if all these tasks are helping you achieve the business's overall strategic goals and company-wide vision?

Companies invest in many tools and processes to complete projects on time. However, unless you have accountability and can connect your strategy to unified key business objectives, your company can't make true progress.

In many organizations, the right-hand does not know what the left hand is doing. As an organization grows in size, this issue can become even more prominent. That's perhaps one of the main reasons that startups have a track record of being nimbler and more innovative.

When there is a lack of alignment at the highest levels in any organization, that usually trickles down the hierarchy. For example, imagine that you're launching a new rocket into orbit. With such a high-stakes project, you would need to be sure about every minute detail of the launch program. If the launch angle is even one degree off, then the rocket's trajectory and end destination will be miles off. An organization like SpaceX takes months (and possibly years) to plan, coordinate, and execute a successful rocket launch; and these projects cost sometimes as high as a billion dollars. It's often an extensive process that requires exact alignment between every department.

While projects in your business may not require the precision of launching a rocket, a lack of alignment between even two departments in your business could push your progress back weeks or months.

Most employees in a company will focus on their own goals without understanding how their success impacts the company's overall vision and goals. Your company's vision can often be lost on employees and managers who have narrowed their focus down to their daily to-do list.

Aligning OKRs throughout your entire organization and ensuring that department and team leaders are communicating with one another and referencing the company's overarching goals when setting their own priorities is the best way to keep everyone aligned and achieve more, more efficiently.

Challenges with Commitment

As a leader, you naturally have lofty goals and ambitious visions for a company that you care about. From these goals, you give marching orders to your directors and managers, who then pass it on to front-line employees.

Is that enough to get employees committed to the company's success? You'll notice that everyone cheers for a strong, ambitious vision when it's announced during an all-hands

meeting or your annual retreat. However, in the grind of day-to-day work throughout the quarter, enthusiasm dies off as soon as employees are hit with their full workload.

There is an inevitable drop in morale and buy-in across all employees. In their next 1-on-1s, your employees might report back that timelines for the lofty goals are too ambitious, and they need a higher budget, more time, and additional resources.

Lack of commitment and lack of initiative are definite problems in the workplace, but this is not entirely an employee's fault. If your company's environment has a rigid structure that does not encourage failure and flexibility, it could severely hamper employee engagement. Also, you might already know that pushing your employees to work harder and longer hours does not necessarily mean you will get better or faster results. In an environment where employees are told what to do, no questions asked, there is usually a lack of commitment.

Alternatively, when employees are encouraged to come up with their own approaches, methods, and means, there's higher employee engagement and motivation. Most of the time, it is a mindshare problem. Including employees in the process of creating goals and target timelines can go a long way when it comes to keeping teams committed to their quarterly OKRs.

Google's '20% time' is perhaps one of the most discussed examples of a company giving its employees autonomy and creative freedom to both come up with new ideas, and choose methods to solve problems. Founders Larry Page and Sergey Brin mentioned the 20% time in their 2004 IPO letter, sharing that Google encouraged employees to spend 20% of their working hours on a project or problem of their choice. Some of the most successful Google products such as Google News, AdSense, and Gmail came out of this 20% time from Google employees.

Now, your company may not be able to allot 20% of the team's time towards new projects.

Another effective practice that you can utilize is taking advantage of something called the IKEA effect.

Studies have shown that consumers place a higher value on things they assemble themselves—for example, they value their IKEA bookcase that they built themselves over the ready-made one they bought at the store. This cognitive bias— named the IKEA Effect— can be used to promote employee engagement within your organization. If everything in your company is structured around orders from the top-down, your employees will naturally be less motivated. So, the remedy is simple: give employees more ownership over how they approach the goals teams set. If an individual is assigned a department-level key result as an objective, allow the employee to come up with their own key results to fulfill that goal. This enables leaders to still direct employees, without completely dictating how the employee goes about fulfilling the goal.

Challenges with Measurement

One of the most famous quotes from Peter Drucker, the "father of management thinking" is this: "What gets measured, gets improved."

Even in the age of 5G, AI, and blockchain, this time-tested wisdom is relevant and important. Most companies track certain aspects of their business. Publicly traded companies report their quarterly incomes, forecasts, EBITDA, etc. each and every quarter. Start-ups must report their up-to-date stats and results periodically to their investors. So, there is an inherent understanding of the value of tracking and measuring results among companies of all sizes.

If you don't routinely track your critical KPIs (Key Performance Indicators) accurately, then you won't know if you are actually making progress, or if you're just running in place.

The key to improving any aspect of your business is to:

- Know how to track and measure relevant KPIs periodically

- Set improvement targets for those KPIs and track progress towards them

This might seem simple, but many major issues in business are rooted in straightforward problems that can be fixed, so long as they can be identified.

Challenges with Stretching

Here is a challenge that most companies probably don't even know exists: setting stretch goals. It is especially difficult when, from a leader's perspective, it looks like the organization is healthy and thriving.

To help determine if you are facing this challenge within your business, take a look at the following statements:

- "My organization is satisfied when an employee sets a goal to complete 3 tasks, but ends up completing 4 tasks, thus resulting in a 133% accomplishment rate."

- "My organization is satisfied when a person commits to completing 10 tasks but only completes 7, resulting in an accomplishment rate of 70%."

Which of these is true for your organization? If you answered yes to option one rather than option two, you're facing a bigger issue than you might realize.

In the business world, this strategy is usually referred to as sandbagging, meaning that your team is content to set lower targets for themselves to achieve or exceed rather than higher targets for them to reach for and possibly fall short.

Gold is difficult. Let me just accomplish Silver.

Overachieving on targets does provide a temporary morale boost, and it can be tempting, especially if you are under the watchful eyes of customers or investors. Internally, however, sandbagging will create a comfort zone that can result in wasted time and wasted resources. The worst part of this issue is that you might not even recognize it in your business.

That's why it's important to implement OKRs, which promote stretching as a central pillar of the framework. In this fast-paced globalized economy, you cannot afford to be comfortable and rest on your laurels. As a leader, you have to set stretch goals to ensure that you stay relevant in the marketplace.

So, explain again - Why OKRs?

Let's go back to the question asked at the beginning of this chapter: *Why do I need to adopt OKRs?*

After reviewing the five common problem areas, the answer is apparent. Your business may not face all these challenges, but it is hard to find a company that does not suffer from at least two or three.

You can argue that you have other ways to address some of those challenges. And this is true; OKR is not the only option for a strategy-execution framework. Other methodologies can give you solutions for individual challenges or groups of challenges— but OKR as a framework can comprehensively address these five challenges, and more. Additionally, OKR is used on a quarterly basis, so as your issues and goals develop, so does your solution.

2

How are businesses optimizing their execution?

In younger startups, business = product. We've heard this and similar sentiments in the context of product development repeated over and over during the last decade. This means that if you want your team to have agile development, you must have an agile business.

Larger businesses have been developing and implementing several strategy-execution methodologies over the last several decades to bring focus and alignment to their workforce. These methodologies aim to design, monitor, and operate business processes that enhance customer experience and grow the business.

It's the iteration of hypothesis, changes, and measurement that will make you better at a faster rate than anything else we have seen.

Gabe Newell
CEO, Valve

The Optimization Waves

In the context of larger businesses, there has been a shift from traditional business practices to more modern, optimized ways of doing business. This shift can be categorized into three stages, as demonstrated in Figure 2.1:

- Transaction Optimization

- Engineering Optimization

- Business Optimization

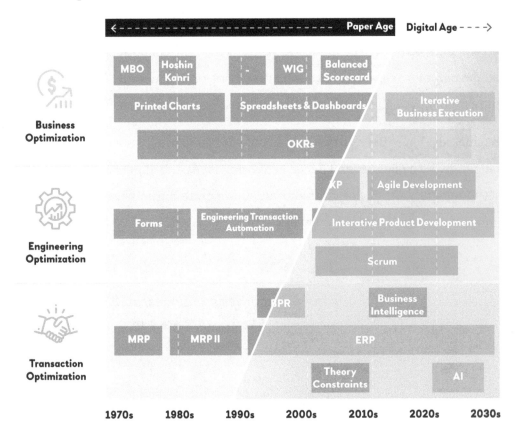

Figure 2.1: The timeline for the three optimization waves.

The Transaction Optimization Wave

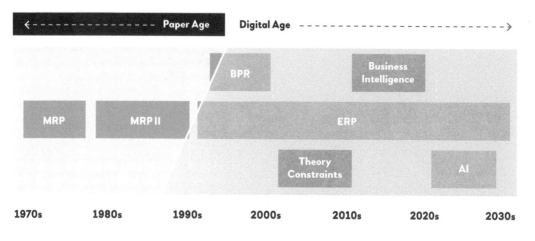

Figure 2.2: Transaction optimization wave timeline

Transaction optimization primarily occured in the 1990s, when ERP, or enterprise resource planning, came to the forefront of the business world. This wave of optimization mainly focused on automating business transactions like receiving materials into inventory, automating financial accounting, bookkeeping, and manufacturing execution, among many other business processes and transactions (Fig. 2.2). These processes all aim to help a business research, make, store, sell, collect, and produce financial reports for a business.

While manufacturing planning and inventory tracking automation was in effect as early as the 1970s, this optimization wave was defined by ERP's inclusion of not just manufacturing, but all aspects of a business.

ERP has acted as the flagship of automation systems. During this optimization wave, the concept of business process reengineering also emerged in a big way. A typical outcome of a BPR (Business Process Re-engineering) exercise is an improved business process that is well supported by an amazing software system.

In many cases, this software system happened to be an ERP system.

Once this wave started, there were several add-ons to the ERP mothership: Human Resource Management, Advanced Planning or Constraint Based Planning, Customer Relationship Management, Business Intelligence, and, more recently, a flurry of AI initiatives to further optimize transactions. This wave focused on reducing or completely eliminating waste in all forms.

Transaction optimization is, naturally, still occuring today– nearly three decades after the advent of ERP. However, even newer optimization waves have eclipsed this automation in the business world.

The Engineering Optimization Wave

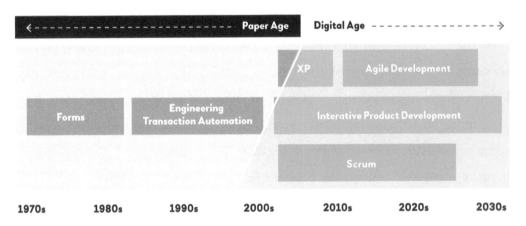

Figure 2.3: Engineering optimization wave timeline

There is some overlap between transaction optimization and engineering optimization. The transaction optimization wave, however, focused mainly on automating engineering transactions such as new product authorizations, engineering change orders, issue tracking or bug tracking, and many such transactions.

In the early 2000s, a shift occurred, bringing attention away from optimizing transactions to optimizing product development. This optimization wave is defined by focuses such as agile product development, extreme programming, and scrum. These shifts generally occurred within companies and startups.

This wave provided the foundation from which iterative product development launched.

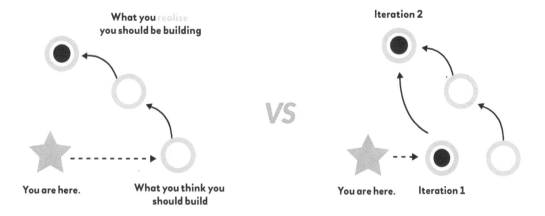

Figure 2.4: *Traditional product development techniques versus iterative product development*

During this phase, many execution methodologies flourished, the most popular of which is scrum, a software development technique that has now evolved into SAFe (Scaled Agile Framework). Enterprises use the scrum approach to develop products with agility, getting them to the market faster without sacrificing quality or taking risks. Scrum enables teams to get fast product feedback, make feature and schedule adjustments, and arrive at their ideal product position sooner, so they can scale faster. Iterative product development techniques quickly became the industry standard for software development (Fig. 2.4).

The Business Optimization Wave

Business management methodologies have been used by companies in all industries for decades. The most famous of these include:

- MBOs in the 60s

- Hoshin Kanri in the 70s, predominantly practiced by Japanese companies

- OKRs since the 70s, practiced by very few companies till the early 2000s

- WIGs, or wildly important goals since the 90s

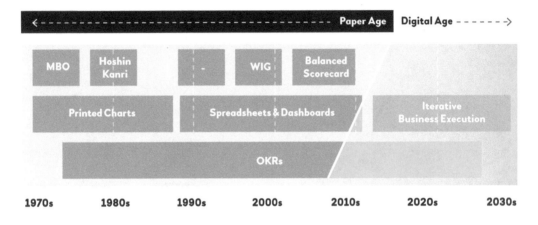

Figure 2.5: Business optimization wave timeline.

However, none of these hit the mainstream until 2000. When companies like Google and other industry leaders began using OKRs in the 90s and 2000s, the OKR framework evolved into a complete "management system" that incorporated "best practices" learned by OKR practitioners and borrowed from other successful methodologies.

Around this time, a few large companies also started creating their own versions of iterative management methodologies. For example, Salesforce.com's Marc Benioff launched a methodology called V2MOM. In Benioff's own words, V2MOM stands for the following:

- Vision helped us define what we wanted to do.

- Values established what was most important about that vision; it set the principles and beliefs that guided it (in priority).

- Methods illustrated how users would get the job done by outlining the actions and the steps that everyone needed to take.

- Obstacles identified the challenges, problems, and issues a team would have to overcome to achieve our vision.

- Measures specified the actual result teams aimed to achieve; this was often defined as a numerical outcome.

Business optimization, as a mainstream movement, started in the mid 2010s (Fig. 2.5). While there were many competing methodologies during this time, OKRs had the broadest adoption because they were adopted by several successful companies. This generated a lot of awareness for the framework, supported by a comparatively large number of OKR practitioners and coaches.

The other main reason for adoption was the availability of many software solutions which helped make adopting OKRs easier and also provided a way to connect the OKR framework to other aspects of the business. The digitization of the OKR process and the integration of OKRs into other key aspects of a business accounts for the uptick in OKR adoption. Teams can certainly start an OKR journey or a WIG journey using spreadsheets and PowerPoints. However, when it comes to scaling OKRs, they'll feel the same pain felt by businesses that were using standalone, non-scalable software in the 80s which pushed them to move towards holistic ERP solutions.

While mastering the OKR framework is not an overnight process, the work is well worth the reward. OKRs, when adopted and used correctly, can bring businesses a host of benefits. These include the ability to:

- **Focus** on the right initiatives

- Ensure everyone involved is **Aligned** with the key focus areas established

- Ensure that you have a **Committed** team behind you

- Establish clear **Tracking** metrics and schedules

- Promote an aggressive culture by pushing your teams to **Stretch** and not treat every initiative as business as usual

Over the years, the OKR framework has evolved into a holistic approach to business management that results in the five benefits of a proper iterative business execution methodology. This framework enables teams to address aspirational goals with iterative execution while also creating committed priority objectives and key results to maintain "business-as-usual".

Engineering Optimization vs. Business Optimization

	Scrum	OKRs
Cycle	Sprint	Quarter
Typical Cycle Duration	2 Weeks	Quarter
Planning Process	Sprint Planning	OKR Planning
Planned Work	Sprint Backlog	Quarterly OKRs
Review Process	Daily Stand-up	Check-ins + weekly group review
Review Cycle	Daily	Weekly
End of Cycle Review	Daily	Weekly

Figure 2.6: Comparing scrum and OKRs

While the Engineering Optimization and Business Optimization waves were different, there are several similarities. Let's quickly understand the similarities between scrum and OKRs, each of which was the most popular approach to iterative execution in its respective optimization wave.

Cycle & Duration

In scrum, a cycle is called a sprint, and the duration of a sprint is usually two weeks. In the OKR framework, a cycle usually lasts a quarter.

Planning Process

In scrum, you conduct a sprint planning process where you go through all the "candidate features" to build, which is called a "product backlog" and decide what can be accomplished in the sprint. This planned work is called the "sprint backlog."

In the case of OKRs you have an OKR planning process where you go through any targets that are still relevant from last quarter's plan, and new key results that need to be added to your OKR list. Once this list is developed, you have your planned OKRs for the quarter.

Review Process

The review process in scrum is called the "stand up meeting" which is held on a daily basis. In the OKR framework, OKR reviews are called check-ins, which are typically held on a weekly or biweekly basis. Check-ins are supplemented by weekly group reviews to share what progress was made during the previous week, the plan for the upcoming week, and discuss any previous or anticipated problems in executing that plan.

End of Cycle Review

The end of cycle review is called sprint retrospective in the scrum methodology. The sprint retrospective is an opportunity for the team to inspect itself and create a plan for improvements during the next sprint. This occurs after the sprint review and prior to the next sprint planning.

In the OKR framework, the end of cycle review is called the OKR reflect and reset. Teams create a structured questionnaire to reflect on what happened in the quarter, documenting and sharing learnings and wins. Then, during the reset portion of this process, teams go back to the drawing board and prepare the plan for the next quarter, having gained knowledge from the previous quarter's OKRs, and under the guidance of the larger business plan or strategy.

3

What is Iterative Business Execution?

There are several similarities between popular methodologies in both the engineering optimization wave and the business optimization wave, at the conceptual level. However, there are several differences between the two groups of methodologies at the operational level. While documenting these differences is beyond the scope of this book, let's learn how to implement an iterative business execution process using OKRs.

Iterative Business Execution

How can you visualize and implement iterative business execution in your business? Following are the key components of iterative business execution:

- Strategy

- OKRs

- Tasks

- Employee Development

- Employee Engagement

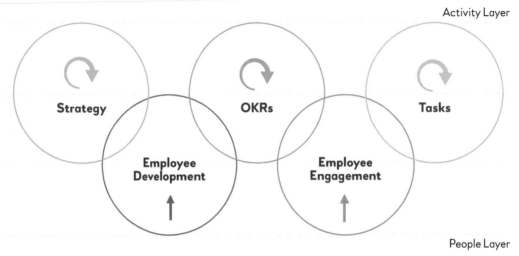

Figure 3.1: The five components of iterative business execution

Strategy

To begin, examine the vision & mission of your enterprise. This should provide the common purpose to rally your employees to pursue your organizational goals with vigor. There are several actions you must take to ensure you have a clear strategy for your business. The list includes the following:

- Establish strategic priorities

- Decide the focus areas or strategic perspectives

- Design initiatives with milestones within these focus areas to achieve the strategic priorities

- Identify strategic KPIs that need to be tracked to measure strategy progress

OKRs

After identifying your strategic direction, create your OKRs. OKRs provide an execution roadmap for your strategy to help you track, report, and adjust execution on a quarterly basis. So how do you go about creating and managing OKRs?

Anchor your Objectives

When you begin your quarter, you need to know what your key objectives are, and ensure that your senior leadership clearly understands and is committed to the OKR framework.

Plan your outcomes for each of these Objectives

In order to unequivocally claim that you have reached your anchored objectives, you need to have tangible results to help you measure your objectives.

A good approach to planning out these measureable or trackable outcomes is to imagine yourself time traveling to the end of the quarter in question, and visualizing what you would like to see improved within your organization. Now, this cannot be a complete dream. It has to be aggressive, but achievable.

Cascade or align your OKRs from the top-down and the bottom-up to establish OKRs at different levels of your business.

Create OKRs for subsequent levels in your business and ensure that employees at every level are clear on what they need to accomplish, how they impact the OKRs of their managers, and how they impact the company's OKRs.

Weekly Check-Ins

Weekly check-ins allow users to:

- Get a pulse check on what is happening with your group's OKRs

- Feed off of each other's successes and get the desired outcome at the end of the quarter

- Share your learnings with others and promote collective problem-solving

- Resolve bottlenecks with dependencies

Business optimization, not department optimization

It's very important to optimize for the success of the business, not just to make a particular department look good. OKR planning and execution needs to provide direction for every employee, but be flexible enough to accommodate changes due to business priorities.

Tasks

Tasks are the engines of daily work. Tasks can refer to a number of things: they could be activities in your CRM system that you perform as part of your outreach, or working on customer-reported issues in your complaint tracking system. Regardless of what the action is, tasks are the "daily management" vehicles that help you achieve the planned key results set for the quarter.

Employee Development

Understanding the developmental needs of employees through conversation and feedback sessions is the final component of iterative business execution. While high-performance organizations rely on employees' initiatives to build the capabilities needed to perform their work, you need to have a process for identifying required skills. Additionally, you must understand your current capabilities and skills gaps, and find innovative ways to fill these gaps, including training current employees, and hiring experts in that field.

This component is focused on individual employees, how they performed in past periods, and how they fit in the long-term plan of the team and company as a whole.

Employee Engagement

Employee engagement is the key ingredient for successful iterations of your business priorities. Total employee involvement needs to be promoted by:

- Acknowledging and recognizing achievements

- Promoting learning & sharing

Engagement doesn't happen automatically. There has to be a conscious effort by the organization to promote engagement. There is no single magic trick here; a collective system needs to be designed and implemented to promote engagement, as increased employee engagement has been directly linked to increased motivation and productivity among employees.

Take advantage of the tools you have at your disposal; have weekly meetings to touch base with employees, or display how employee goals impact larger company priorities so that each employee recognizes that they make significant contributions every day that directly affect the success of the organization.

Habitualize Iterative Business Execution

Institutionalizing and habitualizing iterative business execution is the key to reaping the benefits of iterative business execution. There are a lot of moving parts, and there are a lot of moving parts within those moving parts. This is where complexity sets in.

Not paying attention to this complexity can harm your business. If you thought you could simply write your OKRs week one of the quarter and then revisit them at the end of that quarter to understand what you have accomplished, you are in for a shock. Business iterations require many components to work correctly within a business. Every business is unique, so unfortunately there is no standard template you can follow to ensure that you're getting the most out of the iterative business execution system.

The good news is that you can design your own system that will work for you and will become a competitive advantage for your business. The "not so good news" is that it will take a few iterations for the OKR framework to become a standard practice in your organization. Unfortunately, your organization as a whole cannot perfect OKRs in a month, or even in a quarter. With this framework, patience and persistence are virtues. Demonstrate a strong commitment to this framework, and in about two or three quarters, OKRs will be your most powerful business asset.

It's very important to have a structured, repetitive process that becomes a habit in your organization. Both the concept and process of your own iterative business execution system must be a part of your organizational DNA. New employees should be able to adapt to your iterative business execution process as they onboard without much difficulty.

Why Iterative Business Execution picking up steam?

There are a few key trends that have resulted in the current wave of Iterative Business Execution. Four factors have created the ideal conditions for the Iterative Business Execution tidal wave. These trends feed into each other and add to a much larger whole.

1. Business processes go digital

As broadband and mobile internet at home and work crossed critical thresholds in the early 2000s, key business processes started going digital.

Digital marketing has captured a large share of the advertising dollars as every business wants the ability to precisely target customers and make rapid changes to marketing strategy based on the latest information.

B2C and B2B sales alike are going digital and gaining steam. From books to diamonds and from office supplies to multi-million dollar machinery, both consumers and businesses are embracing online sales at a furious pace. Technology helps companies constantly improve customer-facing processes to remove friction, improve engagement, boost conversions, and increase online sales.

Procurement was one of the earliest business processes to go digital with the establishment of B2B marketplaces and digitization of supply chains. This resulted in increased transparency and visibility across the entire chain.

HR has embraced technology to help with many key processes including hiring, onboarding, training, employee engagement, and performance management.

2. Cloud computing, the great leveler

Cheap storage, processing power, and ubiquitous connectivity have all accelerated the speed that businesses are moving to the cloud. This has helped teams rapidly develop new customer-facing applications and quickly deploy them and test for better customer acceptance and usage.

Until the 90s, businesses and IT used to have an arms-length relationship. Businesses typically had a long wait time to get IT's attention to develop new applications or enhance existing ones to meet their requirements.

3. Faster pace for work and business

Two things have changed in this century. First, the business workforce is now dominated by digital natives who grew up with computers and the Internet and are quite comfortable experimenting with cloud applications for their needs, overriding IT, if required.

Second, the pace of doing business has dramatically increased. Probably the best way to indicate this is through this chart (Fig. 3.2). This shows the time it took for 50 million users to adopt the product or technology listed on the y-axis. As you can see, the amount of time has dramatically shrunk with more recent technology, effectively demonstrating the dramatic changes our world has undergone.

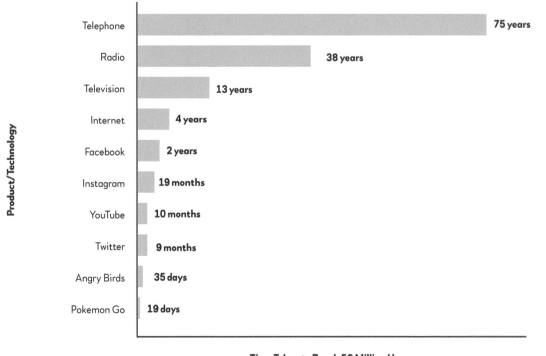

Figure 3.2: *Graph depicting the amount of time it took each type of technology listed on the y-axis to reach 50 million users.*

4. Data-based decision making

The TV show Mad Men showed how advertising decisions were made during the '60s, also known as the golden age of mass media advertising. High-powered, cigar-smoking advertising executives made decisions on multi-million dollar campaigns based on their "hunches". In the 21st century, decision-making is now based on data rather than intuition.

Successful companies like Apple, Amazon, Google, Booking.com, and Expedia conduct thousands of experiments to make informed decisions about where they advertise, who they advertise to, and how often they do it. A/B testing is used to make informed decisions about pricing, user adoption, content, and all aspects of sales marketing.

Adopting Iterative Business Execution is not only for Apple, Amazon and Google anymore

If you think that iterative business execution is only for technology giants like Apple, Amazon, and Google, think again. They became industry-leaders and disrupters because of iterative business execution.

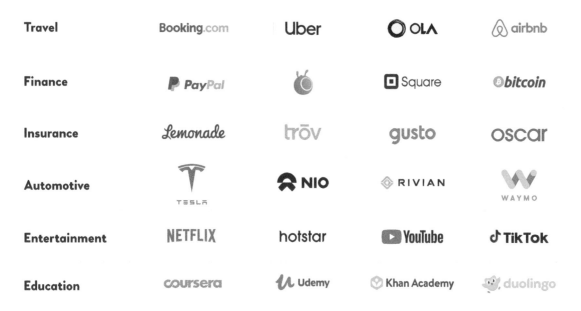

Figure 3.3: Companies that use iterative business execution.

These companies listed in figure 3.3 designed their business models from scratch using technology and processes to embrace iterative business execution. For companies that wish to serve the digital natives and maintain their industry leadership, the choice is clear: adopt iterative business execution, or be prepared to go the way of fax machines and typewriters.

4

What are OKRs?

*Building a visionary company requires one
percent vision and 99 percent alignment.*

Jim Collins
Built to Last

OKRs– The Bridge between Strategy and Achievement of Goals

If you are a business leader, you've probably read a lot about the importance of strategy and the discipline of execution. As the above Jim Collins quote indicates– one without the other is meaningless.

OKRs help teams and companies execute their strategic goals using a well-defined operational framework. OKRs are actively used by the technology titans revolutionizing our 21st century world: Apple, Google, Amazon, Microsoft, Netflix, Twitter, and Spotify, as well as countless start-ups and innovative companies.

What are OKRs?

OKRs are a goal management system used by large and small teams, to collaborate and achieve stretch goals through a framework that requires regular check-ins, continuous feedback, institutionalized learning, collaboration, and problem-solving.

Objectives (the O in OKR) are qualitative, inspirational, and time-bound (typically in a quarter) goals to be executed by a department (say, Human Resources), team (Recruitment), or an individual.

Here is an example of a good Objective:

- Build a high-performance analytics team

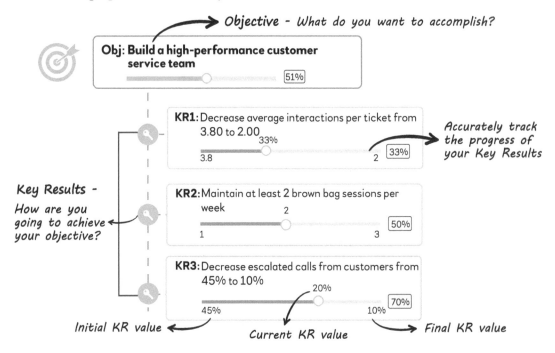

Figure 4.1: A well-structured OKR combines an objective that states what you want to accomplish, and measurable key results that state how you will track the achievement of your goal.

This statement is brief, memorable, and ambitious. It clearly states the goal that the assigned individuals will be focusing on, and there is no ambiguity or confusion.

Key Results (KR), on the other hand, quantify the objective and break it down to specific metrics that can be used to measure the achievement of the associated Objective.

The above Objective can be broken down into Key Results such as:

- KR 1 – Hire 10 new employees for the Analytics team

- KR2 – New team members complete 3 analytics initiatives in their assigned areas, in their first full quarter after joining.

- KR3 – Achieve 90% and above scores on employee satisfaction surveys for new hires

However beautiful the strategy, you should occasionally look at the results.

Sir Winston Churchill

The 5 Key Elements of OKRs

| Focus | Alignment | Commitment | Tracking | Stretching |

Figure 4.2: The five key elements of properly-set and managed OKRs, as defined by John Doerr.

According to John Doerr (the celebrated venture capitalist who popularized the OKR framework), there are 5 key elements of OKRs:

Focus: Companies should define less than five objectives per team or OKR level and between three and five key results per objective. Objectives should also be able to fit in a single line so they are memorable and brief. These limits force organizations and teams to focus on their most important goals and targets. The problems of "multitasking" and dilution of attention have been well documented by productivity experts.

Limiting the number of OKRs at an individual, team, department, and corporate level ensures that individual bandwidth and organizational resources are concentrated on the business's highest priorities, and nothing more. Achieving stretch goals is possible only when individuals and teams give their undivided attention to the few goals that are most important.

Alignment: Research indicates that over 85% of corporate employees are unaware of organizational strategy and goals. OKRs solve this problem by ensuring that the Corporate goals (OKRs) are cascaded to departments and team goals through top-down assignment or bottom-up alignment. Alignment shows how day-to-day priorities are connected to overall company objectives, and can help motivate employees as they see how their work contributes to the company's success. Alignment throughout an entire business can help teams work together better, limit instances where resources are stretched too thin, and ensure that everyone is moving in the right direction, together.

Commitment: Commitments are OKRs that should be achieved without fail in the chosen time-period. (Example: 100% of employees to be given sexual harassment awareness training this quarter). OKRs can promote a sense of accountability and commitment to certain outcomes, especially when they are tracked transparently throughout a company. When each individual within a company can see the OKRs others are responsible for, there's a greater sense of employee engagement and commitment to meeting targets.

Tracking: OKRs should be tracked on a weekly basis. The metrics for the various key results are established at the beginning of the quarter and should be updated each week to monitor progress. OKRs should be tracked transparently. While this can increase employee engagement and motivation, it also allows for team members to see if others are struggling to meet their targets. This way, peers and managers can offer resources and expertise as required to help get the key results back on track.

Stretching: Finally, one of the key benefits of OKRs is the ability for teams to elevate their performance beyond what they considered possible. This happens when teams set "stretch" OKRs.

All OKRs should be ambitious to help promote growth and drive. For reference, an OKR at 70% achievement is considered "strong performance." An excellent way to encourage employees to set "stretch goals" is to unlink OKR achievement from compensation discussions. Instead, compensation and performance reviews should be based on effort and outcomes— not just the OKR percentage completed.

In life, as in football, you won't go far unless you know where the goalposts are.

 Arnold H. Glasow

OKRs: The Beginning

Andy Grove, the celebrated former CEO of Intel, first introduced the concept of OKRs in the 1970s.

Intel encountered several large competitors like Motorola as they pivoted from being a memory vendor to a microprocessor vendor. The company had to battle against larger rivals in a highly competitive market. OKRs provided an excellent framework for Andy Grove to communicate his goals to the teams across the world. Teams agreed on stretch targets and executed them with focus and alignment.

Andy Grove reviewed progress every week, and early feedback helped teams make quick course corrections. The results were spectacular. Intel beat every other competitor to become the world's leading CPU vendor and, along with Microsoft, has been dominating the IT industry as Wintel. John Doerr worked directly with Andy Grove at Intel and witnessed the power and effectiveness of the OKR framework. Doerr moved on from Intel and became a prominent venture capitalist, mentoring and investing in companies like Google, Intuit, Amazon, Square, Uber, and Zynga.

In 1999, he introduced Google to OKRs when they were just 60 employees. Google has publicly credited OKRs for their phenomenal success. From Google, OKRs spread like wildfire across companies in Silicon Valley and beyond.

Interest in OKRs has surged in the 2010s

As you can see from the Google Trends curve depicted below (Fig. 4.3), the interest in OKRs has been steadily increasing from 2012, surging after 2018 when John Doerr published his best-seller *Measure What Matters*. The widespread success of the book made OKRs a more mainstream framework for businesses, and its popularity has grown even outside of the tech industry.

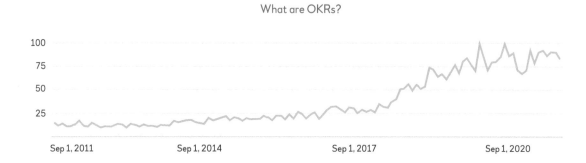

Figure 4.3: Google Trend Curve depicting the increase in searches relating to OKRs around 2012, and the spike around 2018, when John Doerr published Measure What Matters. *Data Source: Google Trends (https://www.google.com/trends)*

In his landmark 2011 Editorial in the Wall Street Journal, Marc Andreessen declared that software is eating the world. He predicted that Silicon Valley-style technology companies would be taking over large swathes of the economy; and as of 2021, companies like Apple, Amazon, Netflix, and LinkedIn have completely disrupted large industries like entertainment, communication, advertising, and recruiting.

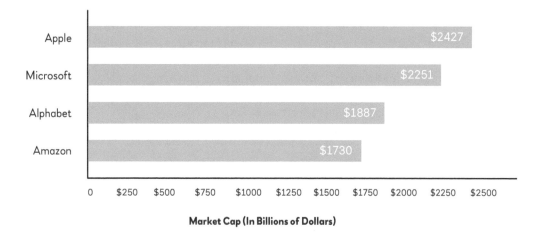

Market Cap (In Billions of Dollars)

Figure 4.4: Graph of top companies and their market cap as of September 2021 **Source:** *Google Finance*

The top four companies mentioned above and almost all the companies referred to by Marc Andreessen have one thing in common: they use OKRs as their goal management system.

As Steve Jobs said about the success of Apple products, the reason OKRs have been gaining widespread adoption compared to the hundreds of other competing management theories is, simply, that "it works."

Comparing Goal Management Systems

	BHAG	WIG	OKR
Name	Big Hairy Audacious Goals	Wildly Important Goals	Objectives and Key Results
Proposed by	Jim Collins in his classic book – 'Good to Great".	Stephen Covey, in his book "The 4 Disciplines of Execution".	Andy Grove Practiced OKRs first in Intel in the 1970s, Introduced to Google by John Doerr in 1999.
Definition	A BHAG is a huge and daunting goal, that is clear, compelling, captures people's imagination and brings teams together to strive towards the finish line.	Wildly Important Goals are the most important goals that can have an outsized impact on the performance of an Organization, Team or Individual. Each business level should have no more than two WIGs.	Objectives are inspirational, directional and qualitative statements, describing the goals to be achieved. Key Results are a set of metrics that help to measure and benchmark the progress towards the objective.
Example	The most iconic example is President John F Kennedy's 1961 declaration that "America should by the end of the decade, land a man on moon and bring him safely back to earth".	Reduce Churn from 15% to 5% in 18 months.	Obj: Improve Product Stability KR1: Ensure all APIs respond within 100 ms KR2: Zero severity one bugs detected in production systems KR3: Achieve Average Page Load time of 3 seconds.

	BHAG	WIG	OKR
Purpose	Communicating clearly ONE audacious goal and laying out the long-term mission.	To help focus on the most important goals at all levels	OKRs (Objectives and Key Results) help individuals, teams and companies to achieve stretch goals through a well-defined framework. The framework helps companies to achieve their strategic vision through OKR cycles.
Timeframe	Long term– will probably be longer than several OKR cycles.	Depends on the goal and the specific circumstances.	Typically, one quarter, sometimes can be 1 year
Availability of Implementation Framework	Does not provide any operational framework for realizing the lofty goal.	Has a high-level framework, but leaves out low-level Implementation details.	Detailed Framework for implementation available.
Usage	Used by many start up founders, CEOs and political leaders to communicate their long-term vision.	There is no specific sector that favors WIGs over other frameworks.	Most widely used goal management system by some of the most successful tech companies of our times and now spreading to other verticals as well.
Tools	Limited or no tools	Limited or no tools	Rich availability of software products for implementation.

Figure 4.5: Chart comparing BHAGs, WIGs, and OKRs

Tips to write good OKRs
Objectives

Objectives should be short, ambitious, and memorable statements that address the main goals you want to achieve. Every team member should be able to recall their Objectives from memory without referring to their app or system.

Here are some examples of top companies and their real objectives:

Figure 4.6: *Objective examples from top companies.* **Source:** *Measure What Matters*

Objectives need to be energizing, not dull. Feel free to use whatever works in your organization and is in sync with your culture. Objectives can use words like "out of this world," "kickass," "wicked," "groovy," "sweet," "fab," and even "super-duper" to describe Objectives.

Key Results

Key results are targets or outcomes that you will be able to measure in your business to ensure that the objective is successful. Be careful not to make your list of key results a task list. Instead, you should look at important business KPIs to measure what metrics will truly show your growth and progress in your company.

Remember to limit the number of key results per objective to between three and five. This helps maintain focus on only the most important outcomes, and ensures that your team is dedicating time, energy, and resources to what matters most.

Here are some of the key results that the aforementioned top companies used to achieve their ambitious objectives:

▶ YouTube	"Grow Kids' engagement and gaming watch time (X watch hours per day)"
(Chrome)	"Achieve 20 million weekly active users for Google Chrome by year-end"
myfitnesspal	"Add 27 million new users in 2014"
BILL & MELINDA GATES foundation	"Sustain current global progress to ensure the environment is Conducive to eradication push"

Figure 4.7: Key result examples from top companies **Source:** *Measure What Matters*

Final Thoughts

While there are hundreds of management theories and frameworks, the widespread adoption and innumerable success stories of OKRs prove that the OKR framework is powerful and can help companies and teams across all industries achieve more.

OKRs combine a number of crucial elements to help users of this framework achieve their goals. During the OKR planning process, OKRs at higher levels of the company are cascaded to department and team levels, allowing for company-wide alignment and employee empowerment.

Transparent progress tracking, regular reviews, and continuous feedback cycles provide the necessary support and communication needed to achieve ambitious stretch goals. With these elements, it's no wonder that OKRs have powered some of the most innovative companies of this century.

What are OKRs?

5

We frequently review employee performance. Aren't we already iterating faster?

For those unfamiliar with the OKR framework, it might sound the same as a performance management system. Tracking outcomes on a quarterly basis does provide employee-specific data about projects worked on and outcomes achieved. However, there are key differences between performance reviews and OKRs.

The Definition of OKRs

OKRs have increasingly become one of the principal ways for companies to organize teams, giving them ambitious objectives, and providing a specific and actionable road map to achieve them with clear key results. OKRs, or Objectives and Key Results, are management methods that break down a company's objectives into time-bound, achievable actions known as Key Results.

The Definition of Performance Management

Performance management focuses on how employees perform relative to the expectations set for their grade or position. The cycles are usually annual, and the cadence happens through an exercise called yearly (or annual) performance reviews.

The Differences between OKRs and Performance Management

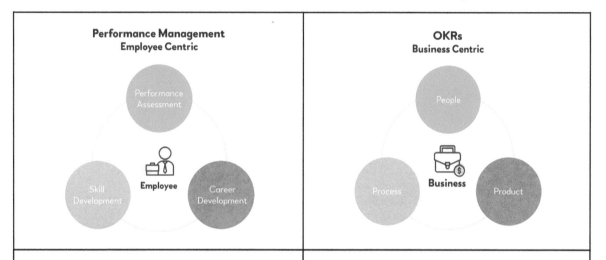

Performance reviews focus on an employee.	OKRs are business-centric.
The emphasis is on how their skills match up to their job requirements, and it includes (but is not limited to):	OKRs define what an individual, team, department, or a business as a whole needs to accomplish in a particular quarter, and how they measure their progress towards achieving what they are trying to do.
· How to make them better at doing their current job.	As they achieve those results, the general expectation is that the business will do better as a whole in terms of customer satisfaction, revenue, product quality, supplier satisfaction, or any other factor that makes the company move forward.
· Realigning their career aspirations periodically.	
· Helping them with their career path through coaching, training, and sponsored higher studies.	
Also, performance management helps identify those employees who lack the skills to perform their job. If there is no visible path to make the job fit the employee, determine a future course of action, including termination.	

Figure 5.1: Chart comparing performance management and OKRs.

Here are a few areas where Performance Management and OKRs differ:

- Key Focus

- Typical Cycle

- Compensation

- Transparency

Key Focus

OKRs focus on business results (or corporate objectives), while performance management focuses on how employees perform their job. Objectives and Key Results as a strategy-execution framework are centered around achieving outcomes. Meanwhile, traditional performance management tends to focus on output and individual employee productivity.

Because of this difference, it's difficult to use OKRs as a sole means of evaluating performance. Instead, it's better to approach performance reviews from a holistic perspective and make OKRs just one part of your management system.

Typical Cycle

OKRs and performance management differ in their typical cycle as well. OKRs have a shorter timeline (usually three months, or one quarter) to measure and assess goals. Meanwhile, performance reviews are generally very involved and are typically performed once a year.

How does the cycle start for OKRs?

- Corporate, departmental, or team OKRs are established at the beginning of the quarter

- Individual OKRs are created and aligned with one of the company's higher-level OKRs

- Dependencies with other individuals, teams, or departments are discussed and recorded through OKRs

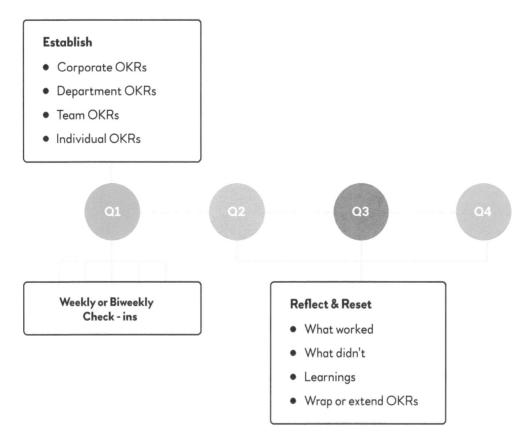

Figure 5.2: *Standard flow of an OKR program.*

How does the cycle end for OKRs?

- At the end of the quarter, teams, departments, or employees share their learnings on the progress they made on their OKRs.

- For each OKR, the team, department, or employees assess where they are, wrap up the OKR as is and mark it complete, or extend it to the next quarter based on business needs.

- Besides OKRs that are extended to the next quarter, new OKRs are added at each level again based on business needs.

How does the cycle start for performance management?

- The Human Resources (HR) department kicks off the assessment cycle after each review period. Review periods commonly last one year or six months.

- Depending on the employee's role within the organization, they will be rated on a set of competencies according to their job performance.

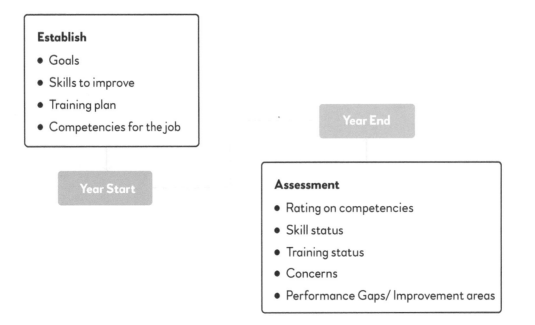

Establish
- Goals
- Skills to improve
- Training plan
- Competencies for the job

Year Start

Year End

Assessment
- Rating on competencies
- Skill status
- Training status
- Concerns
- Performance Gaps/ Improvement areas

Figure 5.3: Typical performance management cycle.

How does the cycle end for performance management?

- The HR department kicks off the assessment cycle.

- Employees perform self-assessments.

- Confidential 360-degree feedback is collected from peers and subordinates.

- The reviewed employee's manager rates the employee on competencies identified for their job role.

- The manager & employee meet and discuss their ratings and complete the review. Any potential disagreements are handled through the HR department. Training or coaching opportunities are recorded.

- The performance and professional development goals for the next review period are set.

Compensation

In performance management systems, reviews are usually tied directly to employee compensation. In the OKR framework, progress has nothing to do with compensation discussions. By nature, OKRs are ambitious. To prevent sandbagging and underachieving for the sake of things looking good at-a-glance, any compensation discussions should not involve the success of OKRs.

OKRs

OKRs promote aggressive target-setting and hence should not be used as the sole factor to determine compensation.

Performance Management

Ever since HR became a business function, performance reviews and assessment has been a precursor to compensation revisions.

Figure 5.4: OKRs & Performance Management's role in compensation decisions.

For example, let's assume that in the software engineering department of Acmesoft Inc, John set a target to deliver 10 feature releases, and completed 8 of the 10 with excellent quality. Meanwhile, Jacob set a target to deliver 4 features for the same product release, but completed 5 with excellent quality.

If this was tied into their annual performance reviews, it would seem, based on percentages, that Jacob is achieving more and contributing more to the organization– but based on the target numbers and their progress, it's John.

Transparency

Finally, OKRs and performance management are different because while one is made to promote transparency and accountability, the other is meant to be private.

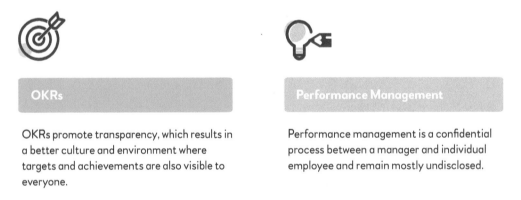

OKRs	Performance Management
OKRs promote transparency, which results in a better culture and environment where targets and achievements are also visible to everyone.	Performance management is a confidential process between a manager and individual employee and remain mostly undisclosed.

Figure 5.5: OKRs & Performance Management's stance on transparency.

Objectives and Key Results should always be transparent. This helps teams maintain full alignment throughout the entire quarter. It also enables higher-level executives and managers to get an at-a-glance overview of who is on track, and who seems to be struggling to meet their targets. If OKRs fall out of alignment, they can course-correct by simply looking into their OKR platform. If some targets are lagging behind, team members will be able to see that and offer resources and assistance as needed.

Meanwhile, performance reviews should not be transparent. An employee's individual performance in their job role, as well as the discussion he or she has with her manager, should be completely confidential. While peer reviewers or subordinates can offer evaluations to contribute to a 360-degree performance review, the discussion should stay between the reviewed employee and their reviewer.

This enables the employee and manager to come up with a performance improvement plan and plan the trajectory of the individual's career without feeling that the entire team is watching or passing judgement.

Final Thoughts

Most individuals (as an employee or a manager) have taken part in some performance management program in their careers. Though they have been useful in managing employee productivity and individual compensation, performance management does not always connect directly to a business's key objectives. There is also the time-delay factor; twelve months is a long time between performance reviews, and it may be difficult for managers to have a productive career discussion with their team members.

Also, as workplaces get more and more diverse with young professionals (Millennials and Gen-Zs) who prefer more candid and frequent feedback, performance management becomes more challenging to implement and manage successfully.

Today's changing workforce wants more visibility and clarity on an organization's goals and a more transparent connection between their contributions and the company's success.

A system like OKRs makes it easier to inform everyone about the company's vision and goals, and helps individuals see how their daily contributions affect the company's OKRs. Performance management certainly has its place in the modern workplace, and will not be phased out by the implementation of OKRs. Instead, OKRs can be used as a complementary methodology to help the company meet its high-priority goals.

6

What does success look like?

Before you are able to steer your organization towards sustained growth, it is essential to define what success means to your business. So, what does success look like?

While success is a common concept that many people envision for themselves, it doesn't have

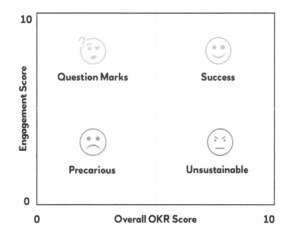

Figure 6.1: A sustainable growth matrix plots departments or companies as a whole based on their engagement score and overall OKR score.

a universal definition. Because of this, you must spend some time considering what success looks like in your specific organization.

To illustrate the definition of success, business leaders can use a sustainable growth matrix, with business results on one axis and employee engagement/satisfaction on the other axis.

On the horizontal axis, there is the overall OKR score, representing what the business has achieved over the defined period. This number is transparent and available to everybody. OKR scores can be on many scales depending on your choice. OKRs are commonly depicted on a 10-point scale.

In general, the score ranges that are generally accepted are:

- **0 to 3** -> Failed to make significant progress.

- **3 to 7** -> Progress was made, but it fell short of the finish line.

- **7 to 10** -> Delivered as planned.

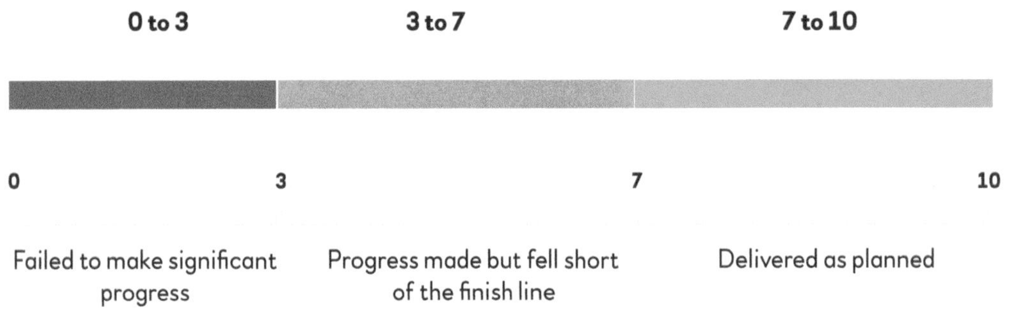

Figure 6.2: Score ranges and their meanings for OKR scores.

On the vertical axis, there is the Employee Engagement score.

The employee engagement score is computed from an eNPS survey.

eNPS is the short form for the Employee Net Promoter Score, which originated from NPS or net promoter score.

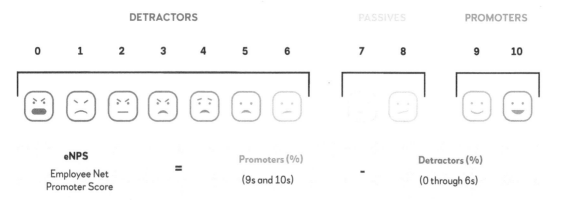

Figure 6.3: eNPS scores and their associated meanings.

In an eNPS survey, you ask employees to agree or disagree with one simple statement: "I would refer this company to my friends to join and work".

The answer is typically on a 5-point or 10-point Likert scale where the lowest number means strongly disagree, and the highest number means strongly agree. The engagement score is simply an average of all the responses, either at the company-level or at the department-level. ENPS respondents are split into 3 different groups: Detractors, Passives, and Promoters.

If you have elected to measure eNPS on a ten-point scale (Fig. 6.3), detractors are individuals who responded between 0 and 6, passives are those who scored at a 7 or 8, and promoters are those who scored at a 9 or a 10.

Where is your company or department positioned?

When you take your company's overall OKR score and the engagement score and then plot it on the matrix, you'll know if you are on a sustainable growth trajectory or if you need to make changes within your organization or strategy in order to course correct.

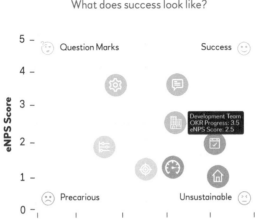

Figure 6.4: Companies plotted on a sustainable growth matrix.

Below are some approaches to getting your business on this sustainable growth path.

An ideal way to get started is to plot your departments or business units in this matrix and see how they fare. If one team or department is noticeably less healthy or sustainable than others, you will know where your focus and resources need to be.

Precarious

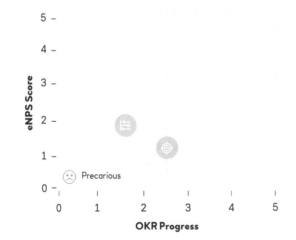

If a department or team has low OKR scores, and low engagement scores, then you know that your business is in a precarious situation.

Not only is this department not achieving the expected business results, but employees are neither motivated nor engaged in their work. Low scores on both axes would place a department in the third quadrant. Businesses in this situation should make significant changes as soon as possible. Higher-level leadership should step in to help department or team leaders clarify goals, realign employees, and promote a more engaging work environment.

Question Marks

If one of your departments has a high engagement score, but a low OKR score, they would sit in quadrant one. This quadrant is called the "Question Marks" quadrant, because employees are reporting high job satisfaction, but low productivity. A team in this quadrant could either mean:

- The targets set through the OKR process were tough, and the department employees are superstars and know that they have got the toughest challenges. They also know that they need to do their part, and the department will see better results in the coming

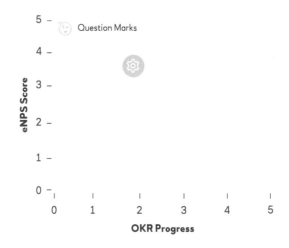

quarters. It is not an ideal situation; however, that could potentially change for the better. Double check OKR targets to determine if this is the issue.

- Another possible explanation is that these employees are not properly trained or informed, and there is a severe information disconnect in your organization. Though their goals are reasonable, there's no substantial progress— employees could misunderstand what they are expected to do, and not realize that their performance is lagging.

When a department or team falls in this quadrant, you should approach the situation carefully and critically. You want to preserve their high engagement and satisfaction, but must figure out why performance is lagging so far behind expectations.

Unsustainable

If a department has a high achievement score on their OKRs, but a low engagement score, they will land squarely in the bottom right quadrant, or quadrant four. This usually means that employees are overworked, and it should be investigated and addressed.

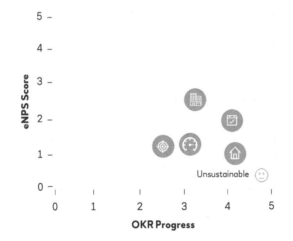

While high achievement levels are something every business leader wants to maintain, they must be supplemented with employee engagement activities. Lack of engagement could come from poor compensation, stressful managerial culture, long work hours, and more.

It may just be that employees are working over their regular hours to get to their high-targets, and do not feel like they are being valued or compensated enough. In this case, it's time to congratulate employees on their hard work, and promote better engagement with bonuses, perks, and positive feedback.

Success

The final quadrant is the sustainable growth or success quadrant, which falls in quadrant two of the graph. Departments land in this quadrant when they have high OKR scores, as well as high engagement scores. This quadrant is ideally where most of your departments, if not your entire business, should be. For most businesses, this is what success looks like; the organization is achieving its goals while employees are highly engaged and motivated.

Final Thoughts

Because OKRs are developed depending on the strategic goals of the organization, and are measured using the KPIs a company has identified as the most important indicators of the business's health, they give users a crystal clear view of organizational progress and success. When you consider OKR progress with regard to employee satisfaction, you might find that your business isn't where you want to be. When your OKR program is managed properly, however, then both OKR progress and employee engagement should increase. So if you find yourself in a quadrant you'd rather not be in, it's time to take a hard look at your OKR adoption strategy.

7

How can you adopt OKRs successfully?

When you are making a process change at your organization or introducing a new methodology, technology can be a beneficial tool and can help you achieve that change. The right software can help you measure, track, and speed up the adoption of a new process or methodology in your organization.

OKR champions and companies that have successfully adopted OKRs will say that the right

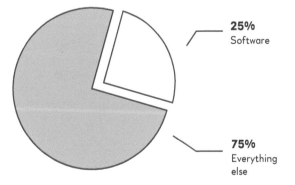

25%
Software

75%
Everything
else

Figure 7.1: Success with OKRs is owed in part to the software used, but mostly to the other practices and processes your business puts in place.

software program contributes to roughly 20-25% of the overall success of the program.

However, the software is just a catalyst, not the most important thing for ensuring that your organization succeeds with OKRs. Many other factors determine the successful rollout of any program— OKR or otherwise. Many businesses start with spreadsheets, and then when they gain more experience and attempt to scale the OKR framework using only Google Sheets or Microsoft Excel, they realize that they need a software program.

It is recommended that you have a clear understanding of that process and what you wish to accomplish. Once you have clarity and also have team and leadership buy-in, then you can confidently go ahead and invest in a software.

Before any business is ready to implement OKRs in their organization, two factors should be considered to help indicate whether or not they will have a successful rollout and implementation:

- The organization's OKR knowledge

- The willingness to learn and invest in best practices

To provide more clarity, look at the simple illustration below. You will see that the grid has four quadrants. OKR knowledge is plotted on the X-axis, and on the Y-axis, there is the willingness to learn or invest in best practices.

An organization's OKR knowledge can range from theoretical (business leaders have just read a book on OKRs) to practical (the team has 6+ months of experience implementing and using OKRs).

In the first six months of an OKR program, spreadsheets or PowerPoint presentations are usually sufficient to keep OKRs transparent and to track key result progress. Of course, a mere month of experience will not make you a superstar or an OKR expert, but you will know

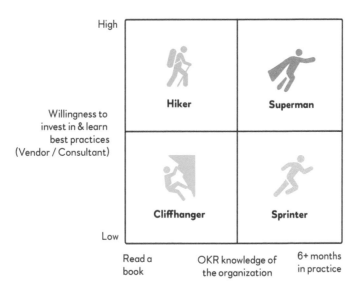

Figure 7.2: *A matrix measuring a business's willingness to learn about OKRs,*
and their history or prior knowledge of OKRs.

enough about the basics, and at this point, you have some comfort in the methodology. The willingness to invest in best practices is mostly about investing money and resources in OKR consultants, who will teach you what to do, what not to do, and how to do it well.

Many OKR experts will tell you that the most significant resistance to the OKR methodology comes from key stakeholders, i.e., the executive or leadership team.

In many cases, some of the suggestions or the best practices are discounted or shrugged off as trivial. For instance, the concept of OKR Scoring is often met with resistance and ridicule. This resistance causes many OKR implementations to go awry. Before you go about rolling out OKRs to your entire organization and purchasing an OKR software, it's imperative to have buy-in from leadership.

There are two ends of the spectrum when it comes to a willingness to buy into the OKR framework: low willingness and high willingness.

Estimating OKR knowledge and willingness can help you tell if your organization is ready to roll out the OKR framework, or if there is more work you need to do before purchasing a software and diving in.

Q1. Cliffhanger Quadrant: Low OKR Knowledge & Low Willingness to Learn

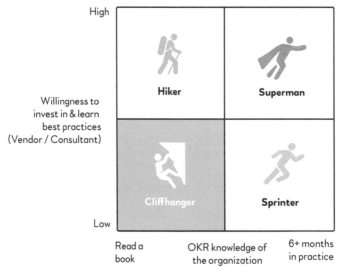

If you are in this bottom left quadrant, your company's willingness to learn and your prior knowledge concerning the OKR framework are both relatively low.

This territory is called the Cliffhanger Quadrant. It is tough to adequately help a company that is in this quadrant. The company's perspective can be summarized with the following: "We don't know much about OKR, but we are also not that open-minded in learning and adopting new ideas."

Every OKR consultant, practitioner, or software vendor has seen clients in this quadrant. With clients like this, it is best for consultants to start by identifying who in the organization is receptive, and if they can help get a broader buy-in within that company.

Here is a typical scenario. A manager or an executive has recently read a book or has attended a conference where she learned about the benefits of OKRs. She is excited about this being a potentially game-changing idea that can help move her company forward. However, when she tries to launch this within her company, she is met with resistance, and the rest of the executive team is not as excited or receptive as she is.

Note that if you identify that your company is in this quadrant, you should first work on demonstrating the value of OKRs and getting the buy-in of the rest of your team. Once your team is at least willing to listen and learn, you can move forward with your OKR journey.

Q2. Hiker Quadrant: Low OKR Knowledge & High Willingness to Learn

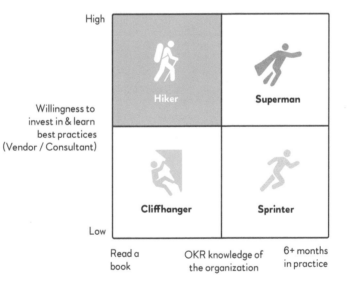

Teams in this quadrant have limited knowledge of OKRs but they are willing to listen, learn, and adapt. Working with these clients is a consultant's dream.

It's encouraging for consultants when clients say, "*We really need some help, and we would gladly invest some reasonable time and resources up front and learn from OKR experts. Can you give us some good advice on who would be the best consultant, or if you're able to do it, what would you do?*"

It's a consultant's job to listen to them, understand their level of expertise, and assess what kind of help they will need. A reliable consulting engagement can be a significant investment for most companies. These experts and consultants are usually in high demand and charge a premium for their expertise; however, the benefits of this consultant outweigh the costs for many organizations. Whether OKR users choose to learn the framework themselves or invest in a consultant, the most important thing for a successful OKR program is a strong willingness to learn.

Q3. Sprinter Quadrant: High OKR Knowledge & Low Willingness to Learn

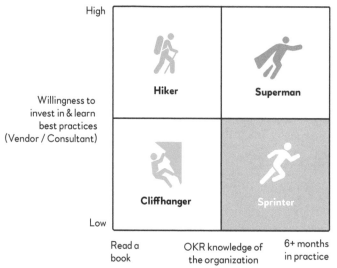

Teams in this quadrant are not worried about industry best practices or benchmarks, because they have first-hand experience on what works and what does not in their company and have committed themselves to that particular way of practicing the OKR framework. At this point, it is mostly a software selection problem for them.

These clients have an inherent knowledge of their OKR journey. They're able to provide details about their OKR program and make it that much simpler for consultants to provide great advice. So, consultants enjoy working with customers in this quadrant. They are off to the races and need a software or tool to help them execute their OKR vision and methodology; they decide what to do, and what features to turn on and off in their initial stages.

Q4. Superman Quadrant: High OKR Knowledge & High Willingness to Learn

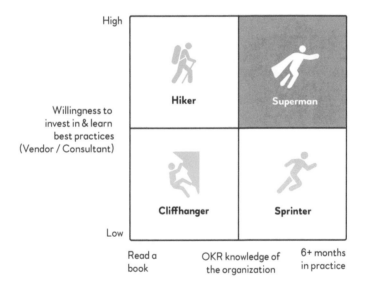

For an OKR consultant or a software vendor, clients in the fourth quadrant are an absolute delight. When somebody is in this quadrant, they have an established OKR practice and are also willing to listen and learn new ideas.

It usually leads to a win-win situation for both the client and the consultant; hence, it's called the Superman Quadrant.

Like the superhero himself, teams in this quadrant will fly through their OKR implementation because they are coming with the right tools and prior knowledge, as well as a strong willingness to adapt and keep learning. Teams in this quadrant will see the benefits of a strong software program and the OKR methodology sooner than their counterparts in other quadrants.

Final Thoughts

In summary, the success of the OKR framework within your organization is largely dependent on how your team is willing to approach the implementation. If you do your research and are coming to the table with a strong learning culture already instituted within your company, there's a strong chance you will see excellent results quickly.

Meanwhile, if your team is not willing to learn, there is little that a consultant or even an OKR software can do for you. The OKR framework asks for its practitioners to be agile and adaptable. If a team can't bring those traits to their approach to the methodology, then it is unlikely that they will get to reap the benefits of OKRs.

8

Why should start-ups embrace OKRs?

Resiliency, not perfection, is the signature of greatness.

Jim Collins

Entrepreneurs set audacious goals to change the world. When they have ambitious ideas they throw their money, time, and their life behind those ambitious ideas. With their relentless pursuit and persistent effort, they build a solution to a problem and deliver it to the marketplace. But have you ever wondered how many of them succeed in this pursuit?

According to the Bureau of Labor Statistics, only 56% of startups make it to their fifth year.

Why do startups fail?

Top reasons why startups fail:

- Ignoring the importance of validating ideas.

- Over-engineering the minimum viable product

- Failing to pivot at the right time

- Lack of alignment between teams towards the vision.

Most of the time, founders tend to lose focus and stray from their plans too often, burning too much cash in the process and inadvertently burying their startups. This is why startups need OKRs.

How do OKRs help start-ups stay focused?

Objectives and key results have focus built into their DNA. Because objectives are limited to between three and five per quarter, with only three to five key results per objective, each sector of the business can focus on their top priorities.

The OKR framework is self-regulating and forces you to narrow down your to-do list. Furthermore, the to-do list is not even a to-do list, but instead a to-accomplish list. There is a subtle difference here. To-do focuses on outputs, whereas to-accomplish focuses on results. OKR allows founders and their teams to forecast outcomes, pursue them, and track them relentlessly.

How do OKRs help teams validate ideas?

Founders have to validate their idea before they roll up their sleeves and plunge into developing the product. They have to be sure whether or not customers will happily pay for using their

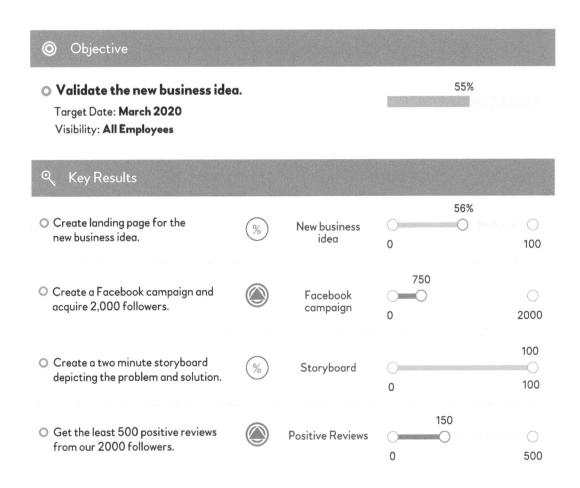

product or the service. Ignoring idea validation will lead them to build something that nobody wants. Without this, start-ups are in danger of wasting time, energy, and other resources developing a solution around an idea, only to find that it's not useful, or doesn't have space in the market.

A simple OKR can help validate product ideas. This OKR is time-bound and will guide the founders to focus on the metrics and work towards achieving the numbers. It will also cut out the execution of new ideas that will pop up in their mind and focus on what matters to reach the Objective.

If the founders achieve these key results, then they could go to the next step of building their prototype. What if they don't meet those numbers? They can reiterate with appropriate modifications based on the feedback that is received from the campaign. If they don't get to their thresholds after multiple iterations, then you can conclude that the market is not ready for the idea and decide that it's not worth pursuing it.

Did you know that Dropbox didn't have a real product in the beginning?

Dropbox is a file storage service used to save and share files across different platforms and operating systems. To get this product done, it requires specialized expertise and a vast amount of resources.

Drew Houston, the founder of Dropbox, created a simple video demonstrating Dropbox in action. It showed how seamlessly it works across different operating systems and uploaded the video to the website. It drove thousands and thousands of people to the website, and their beta waiting list went up from 5000 to 75000 overnight. Anyone who watched the video assumed that the video was a product demonstration, while in reality, there was no real product in existence.

As you can see, it's a lot easier, and much less expensive to test a concept rather than a real product.

How can OKRs help you to build the right MVP?

After testing the idea, you create a minimum viable product. MVP is a prototype of the product, built with minimal features to test the product and to see how customers interact with it.

In traditional product development, developers tend pick up any good idea that strikes them. Sometimes these ideas are misconceived to be useful features, and the development team might as well want to incorporate these into the MVP.

This act of adding a new feature out of the blue to the planned modules will push the release dates further away from the scheduled time. If startups consume more time, only to produce trivial features, you are giving an edge to your competitors. It takes discipline to narrow down the objectives.

To understand this a little deeper, it's important to understand the Big Rock Theory. This theory suggests that to have significant results, individuals must prioritize and give importance to critical activities before dealing with less important activities.

When you use OKRs to develop an MVP, you can create a focused list of features and execute them. OKRs can prove very handy for startups at this stage. OKRs can help startups in the following ways:

- Help all the teams to focus on the customer problem and your solution to that problem.

- Provide guardrails in the process of creating the prototype with minimal, but completely necessary features

- Avoid those features that are helpful and useful, but need not make the cut for the MVP. You can easily sell them as roadmap items.

Here is an example of how a startup can set up their OKR:

This OKR, or some version of it, will help the team deliver an MVP to the marketplace at the earliest possible date. It will keep the team laser-focused on essentials and avoid doing activities that may arise out of their own perceptions and preferences.

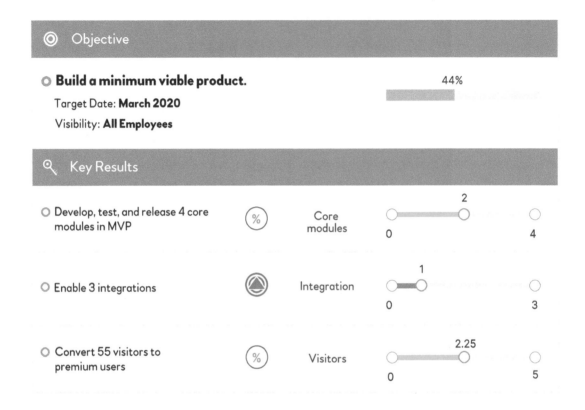

How can OKRs help you pivot at the right time?

The main goal of MVP is to test how the market reacts to your product. You should gauge customers' behavior, analyze your MVP's performance, and measure the results.

MVP results could be measured as:

- New sign-ups

- New premium users sign up

Or any other measure through which you can measure the success of the MVP.

Comparing the results against your expectations will provide confidence and direction to your next iteration of the product. It will not only save your startup from building something that nobody requires, but it can actually guide you on the critical path to something that everyone wants, without wasting time or resources.

Measuring outcomes coupled with customer feedback will help in deciding whether to continue to scale the project or to pivot. Assuming you build your MVP and pivot at the right times using OKRs, you'll be well on your way to running your startup in the most effective and efficient way possible.

9

How can OKRs help remote performance?

What you get by achieving your goals is not as important as what you become by achieving your goals.

 Zig Ziglar

The COVID-19 pandemic has changed how businesses work. Companies have had to go remote, and even as the pandemic dies down in some areas of the world, a hybrid working model is the new normal.

While many companies have taken these changes in stride and adapted well in the circumstances, the downside of working remotely is that team members don't know what their teammates are doing. In this sense, all employees run the risk of being left out of the loop. So managers have to check in with their team often and must communicate clearly to the members in order to manage and improve remote performance.

Setting OKRs for remote teams is a good way to ensure all employees are on the same page, there is no miscommunication, or confusion, thus making performance tracking more manageable– even during remote work.

How can setting OKRs benefit remote performance?

Setting OKRs can benefit remote performance in the following ways:

- Increases focus towards achieving goals

- Boosts productivity of the remote team

- Helps align goals

- Promotes accountability

- Creates a system for regular check-ins

- Builds trust with transparency

1. Increases focus towards achieving goals

OKRs help set clear expectations. And when there are clear expectations set, it helps remote teams prioritize tasks and use resources primarily for those high priority tasks, instead of wasting energy on less important items that might 'seem' important.

It's easy for ambiguity to creep in while working remotely. OKRs take the guesswork out, especially in a remote scenario, and provide more clarity on what the company's top priorities are. Employees are more motivated when tracking progress with OKRs. This concerted effort and focus helps them, their team, and the whole organization scale new heights.

The other benefit of focusing on high-priority tasks and desired results is that remote performance is no longer tied to work hours. Instead, it is based on result-oriented goals, where the team focuses on making progress on their goals.

2. Boosts productivity of the remote team

OKRs boost productivity levels of the remote team. Setting goals that are challenging but achievable pushes the remote team out of their comfort zone to achieve more. The aim must be to achieve 60%-70% of the target. Meeting 100% of the objectives means that the goals need to be more challenging.

3. Helps align goals

Every employee should be aware of what the company's strategy and goals are, and what is expected of them in actualizing those goals. However, things can quickly fall apart due to a lack of clarity and supervision while working remotely. OKR is the glue that holds it together and helps align goals across the company, making sure that performance does not suffer just because the team is remote.

Senior management sets the high-level OKRs, and teams define their own OKRs in collaboration with their managers. Individual and team-level OKRs should tie back in with the larger company-level objectives. The OKR framework encourages users to cascade goals from the top-down, as well as roll up goals from the bottom-up.

Despite the fact that goals are set on different levels, all OKRs in an organization should remain visible to everyone involved throughout the entire quarter. So, regardless of whether or not teams are working remotely, they still very much collaborate and work together, thanks to OKRs.

Continuous effort – not strength or intelligence – is the key to unlocking our potential.

Sir Winston Churchill

4. Promotes accountability

When remote employees are given all the information they need for them to achieve their goals and make their own decisions to achieve them, there is no ambiguity. Sharing all that information is also a display of trust, which can be incredibly motivating, especially in a remote situation where you can't even meet in person. If the company can get its employees motivated, there is no need for micromanaging and nobody has to worry about a lack of accountability.

Since teams set OKRs collaboratively, there is more interest and a sense of accountability for the goals they have agreed on. Weekly check-ins ensure that work and performance run like a well-oiled machine.

5. Creates a system for regular check-ins

OKRs can help remote teams set up a system for their top priorities. Managers and leaders can review team performance on a regular basis using OKR check-ins. Check-in frequency can be adjusted to cater to the team's and organization's needs.

This allows remote teams to communicate more frequently and seamlessly about all aspects of remote performance: how things are going, what's going well, what needs improvement, and what doesn't need to be done at all. This keeps everyone updated on every individual employee's progress, and reinforces the most important goals. The idea is to put goal progress at the top of everyone's mind, giving them the freedom to work on their own schedules and in their own styles, but bringing everyone back to check-in and compare progress at the same time.

OKRs act as a great leveler among different styles of work. It's a great way to get the best out of both introverts and extroverts and for them to share the same platform.

6. Builds trust with transparency

OKRs give a platform for remote teams to converse with each other, be transparent, and stay aligned across teams.

Using an OKR software enables transparency throughout an entire organization, across all levels of hierarchy. Every employee has visibility into their co-workers' OKRs, even when they're working remotely. This cultivates teamwork across the company. Since it is so transparent, every employee is able to see how a co-worker's or a manager's OKR can impact their individual work.

For the managers, OKRs help remotely supervise performance and ensure work is on track, eliminating the need to micromanage.

3 steps to set OKRs for remote teams:

Following are a few steps to set OKRs for remote teams:

Step 1: Introduce the remote team to OKRs

For the OKR approach to work, it is important that everybody is in agreement. Management must clearly state to the remote team why OKRs are being introduced, including sharing the

Step 03
Managers should help remote employees set and execute individual OKRs to teach them the ins aand outs of the framework.

Step 02
Leaders should unambiguously communicate what the company objectives are and show employees how to align their own goals.

Step 01
Management must clearly introduce the remote team to OKRs and share the benefits of the framework.

OKR payoffs or benefits, how it can boost remote performance, and how it can be used to measure success and make strategic decisions. Make sure that all questions are answered regarding OKRs.

Step 2: Communicate clearly what the company objectives are

Once everyone is on board regarding the OKR approach, the next step is to clearly communicate what the company objectives are at the corporate level, so that remote teams are aware that their individual and team goals need to be aligned with the company goals.

It's easy to lose sight of the bigger picture while working remotely and not on site.

Here are a few questions to think about when establishing OKRs for remote teams:

- Does everyone have one big collective goal?

- Are the goals of the employees and teams in sync with the goals of the company?

- Will the team goals help the company meet its OKRs?

- Is there anything that team members need to change about what they are working on?

Step 3: Set and execute individual OKRs in collaboration with the remote employee

It is very important that while setting OKRs for remote teams, managers do it in collaboration with the remote employee. This is especially important since the employee needs to understand how OKRs will help them with their goals, and how it will contribute to the organization.

They need to realize that OKRs are not just a tool to evaluate remote performance; there's so much more to the OKR framework. When they are fully convinced of the benefits of OKRs, they will be more willing to take risks, think outside the box, and be more accountable.

Final Thoughts

Setting OKRs for remote teams offers the perfect balance between performance and supervision. Transparency helps employees take accountability and find the motivation to achieve their goals. Communication is key, and more important than ever when it comes to remote performance. OKRs provide context and meaning to daily work, helping employees stay focused, collaborate, and coordinate with each other to achieve their goals.

10

Are OKR tools better than OKRs with spreadsheets?

*Adaptability is about the powerful difference
between adapting to cope and adapting to win.*

 **Max McKeown**

Many executives within small and medium businesses will identify nimble startups as their primary threat. All business leaders want their team to stay on the cutting edge of productivity and optimization, and of course execute strategy with ease.

To compete with these start-ups, SMBs are adopting OKRs in droves. However, many companies elect to manage their OKRs on spreadsheets, rather than on software. Long story short, many have tried, and many have failed. Let's take a look at an SMB leader's account of what managing an OKR program on Excel Sheets looks like:

- The department leaders briefed their teams about OKRs and gave them general guidance about defining their OKRs and aligning them with corporate and other departments.

- Managers and Individual contributors attempted to define the OKRs in an Excel template.

- Users had difficulty entering their OKRs in the template, and several errors came up.

- People started maintaining multiple versions and were sharing the spreadsheets via emails.

- Some people complained that their OKRs had been "overwritten" by others.

- Objectives and Key Results that had dependencies were especially difficult – for example, "Creating a great Marketing Analytics team" was an important OKR for the Marketing team, while HR did not have " Hiring a great Analytics talent" as their OKR – Both the departments were working with their own Excel sheets, in different offices.

- Cascading or rolling up goals was just not possible– as the planning deadline grew nearer, people were just trying to get their OKR drafts over with. People had a hard time relating how their work impacted others, and even their own department.

- Managers and contributors started complaining about how the exercise was laborious and sucking up a lot of their time.

- Managers who had to report their progress to the CMO had a particularly difficult time; they had to start preparing several weeks ahead of the meeting to collect the Excel sheets from various teams, clean-up the data and create reports for the CMO, making the reports outdated by the time the meeting took place.

- The CMO's experience was not great either – she had to wait for the review meetings to get a sense of the progress of various teams and had to rely on custom reports prepared for the occasion. These reports did not have drill through capabilities and were static. More importantly, these reports were given once a month, and hence there was no way to give early feedback to the teams.

- When a survey was conducted about the OKR implementation about a quarter into the effort, words like "miserable" and "frustrating" were the most common responses.

- The initial enthusiasm about OKRs was replaced with wariness and there was a danger of people associating their frustration with spreadsheets as "inadequacy of OKRs".

- The primary objective of creating a nimble execution team was far from being achieved.

- The CMO and the leaders decided to end their experiment with spreadsheets and adopt an OKR software for the third quarter.

Issues at Different Company Levels

As the above example illustrates, using spreadsheets for your OKR implementation is not a desirable experience for individual users.

To summarize, the issues with spreadsheets are:

For Individual Contributors:

- Cumbersome to enter data into

- Limited scope for aligning their OKRs with other departments and teams

- Easy to make errors and duplicate entries

- Limited visibility of all OKRs

- Lack of timely feedback from managers and other team members

- No easy integration with Task Management and Project Management tools (like Jira and Azure DevOps), causing users to have to re-enter data, negatively impacting productivity.

Overall: OKRs on spreadsheets create a frustrating user experience.

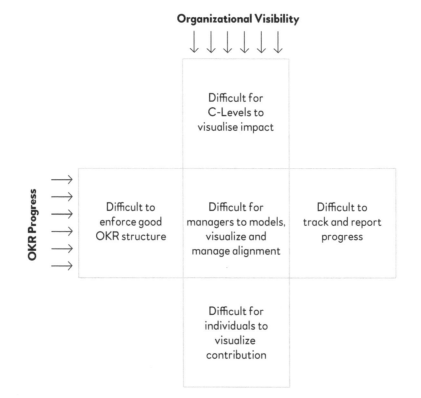

Figure 10.1: *This chart demonstrates the issues that different levels of the organization face when using spreadsheets to track OKR progress.*

For Managers and OKR Champions:

- Scoring errors are rampant.

- Grading OKRs can be difficult.

- Reporting and Reviews can be a chore and can be done only as monthly cadence.

- Maintaining the integrity of the weekly check-ins can be challenging.

- Maintaining the "Conversations, Feedback, and Review" framework inside the spreadsheet cannot be done.

- OKR champions have limited capabilities for setting preferences, visibility, access control and even limited administration of users and departments.

For the CXOs:

Getting a clear picture of the state of business at any given moment is not possible while executing OKRs with spreadsheets as the reports are always dated.

Getting early warning signs of problems will be difficult as issues are hidden within spreadsheets and don't stand out.

Giving timely feedback and early interventions on problem areas is an issue and hence using spreadsheets can defeat the purpose of implementing OKRs.

When business needs demand the cancellation or modification of objectives, making changes while using spreadsheets is next to impossible.

Spreadsheets can still be used by small teams, particularly for planning

Spreadsheets have been used from the early days of computing for various applications such as: simple lists, budgets, data storage, data cleaning, graphs and charts, financial modeling and statistical analysis. Spreadsheets can still be used by small teams (ten or less) for the limited purpose of planning their OKRs. They can define the corporate OKRs, a few departments' OKRs (as long as they use a simple hierarchy) and connect OKRs to tasks, but even with a small team, they will still run into all the issues mentioned above.

Final Thoughts

The verdict is clear: using spreadsheets to implement OKRs does not serve the needs of a serious organization or any type of user– CXOs, department heads, managers or individual contributors.

With so many SaaS-based OKR softwares available, there is really no reason for companies to get stuck with spreadsheets. Using a great intuitive OKR software can increase the enthusiasm of teams and help them stay productive and execute with focus and alignment. Instead of worrying about the problems associated with spreadsheets, team members can spend quality time on defining stretch targets, innovative ways to achieve them, and keep their focus on execution.

11

How does the OKR framework compare to the Balanced Scorecard?

Businesses are established with one thing in mind: growth. All companies– whether they are large enterprises or garage start-ups– strive to expand their business and earn more revenue. Increasing production and skillful marketing are major drivers of success. And since any organization is made up of its employees, creating an uplifting environment for your employees is the key to ultimately growing your business.

Managing your team's performance can greatly enhance your business. The objective and key result (OKR) framework and Balanced Scorecards are evaluation systems that grade the performance of the employees. They both focus on morale-boosting and engagement to increase the efficiency of your team.

What is a Balanced Scorecard?

The Balanced Scorecard, often abbreviated as BSC, is a strategic management system that organizations use to highlight what they intend to accomplish, connect daily tasks to overarching strategy, prioritize projects, and measure progress towards their most important targets.

Balanced Scorecards aim to achieve goals by monitoring four static categories. These 4 aspects of the Scorecard are interrelated to each other. They are Financial Aspect, Internal Process Aspect, Learning and Growth Aspect, and last but definitely not the least, Customer Aspect.

How the Balance Scorecard Links Performance Measures:

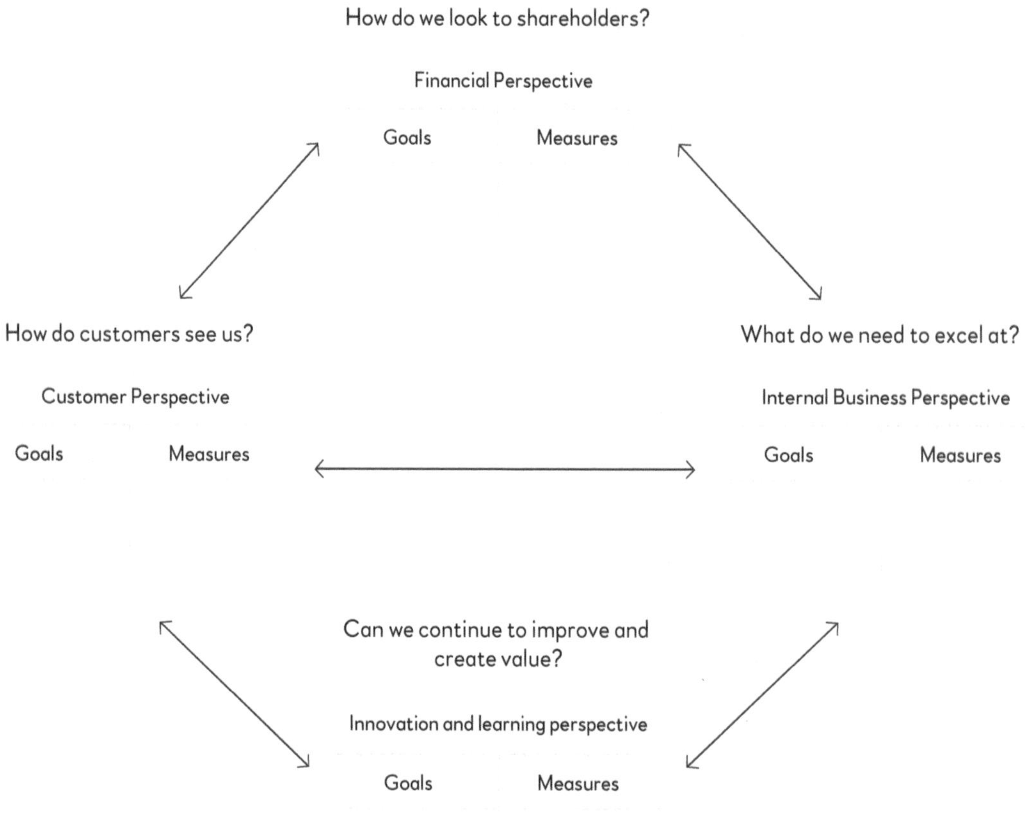

How do we look to shareholders?

Financial Perspective

Goals   Measures

How do customers see us?   What do we need to excel at?

Customer Perspective   Internal Business Perspective

Goals   Measures   Goals   Measures

Can we continue to improve and
create value?

Innovation and learning perspective

Goals   Measures

Figure 11.1: How the balanced scorecard links performance measurements.

All "goals" must be fitted into one of the features. Once the goals are set, users must set "measures" in order to achieve the targets. Then, an "initiative" must be outlined, and an "indicator" of success must be determined. With all of these elements correctly added, the BSC looks something like this:

As you can see in the above image, each aspect of the BSC is connected. Since there are so many bodies functioning at the same time, you can have multiple goals set.

Objectives and Key Results

Objectives and Key Results is a powerful and agile goal-setting framework that allows individuals and teams to stretch productivity beyond what they thought possible.

As we've learned in this book, OKRs are commonly set on a quarterly basis, and users should define no more than 3-5 Objectives per department, team, or individual users. Objectives are statements that are general, ambitious, and memorable, capturing the most important goals that the group wants to achieve in a given quarter. Then, these objectives are made quantifiable using key results. There should be no more than 3-5 key results for each objective defined. Key results must be measurable or trackable outcomes that are mutually exclusive and collectively exhaustive. The key result list, when completed, signals that the attached objective has been fulfilled.

With OKRs, the team members decide what is important and what will be focused on first. Instead of having to align expansion plans with set standards from before, OKRs provide you with more control over your concept. The idea is to have a more streamlined version of project progress.

Objectively Different

While OKRs and BSCs are both tools to manage and oversee performance or productivity, there is a significant difference between these two frameworks. And this difference comes in their strategies.

With a Balanced Scorecard, you must form a strategic map to attain your goals, separated into four parts. Each part of Finance, Customer, Internal Process, and Learning and Growth comes with goals. So, a BSC can have 10-15 goals at one time. The success of each sector can be measured by the achieved goals. It is also a holistic approach.

To understand how it works, for example, consider this table for an app development company:

	Objectives	Measures	Initiatives	Indicators
Financial	Increase revenue	Revenue should be 20% higher than the previous year	Take in better sales and marketing strategies	Financial statement
Internal Processes	Create teams with different expertise	Certified workforce must increase by 50%	Train and certify employees	Employee report
Customer	Increase number of customers	Increase customer by 10% of the previous year	Provide better customer service and experience	Customer feedback
Learning and Growth	Establish an agile workflow	Train team to be cohesive and efficient	Hold training sessions every week in an agile workflow	Team reports

Figure 11.2: *This chart demonstrates how a balanced scorecard breaks down goals.*

OKRs are usually top-down processes; they focus on the bigger picture first and cascade down to measurable targets. By limiting the number of OKRs per team to 3-5 per quarter, employees are not overburdened, and teams can avoid having unbalanced OKR progress. It also provides employees with autonomy and lets them decide on what to focus on first.

For example, consider the same app development company using OKRs:

The company has decided to implement OKRs. Therefore, the main objective will be reached by setting target outcomes, or key results.

Where can OKRs be used?

OKRs are a method of constant tracking for your employees. Regular updates are provided with the use of this framework that help keep everyone up-to-date and fully aligned. Industry-leading companies such as Google and Twitter use this system as a way to keep people informed of the company's top priorities and increase employee engagement. OKRs can work as a major morale-booster as teams see they are making a real impact in their organizations. Additionally, teams can feel satisfied and fulfilled as they check-in key results with continued weekly progress.

Where can BSC be used?

If you aren't focused on process and weekly engagement, OKRs can feel very specific. Companies that want to illustrate end-goals use BSCs. While OKRs are used for regular updates and reviewed every quarter (sometimes every month depending on the business model), BSCs are more effective in envisioning the final destination. They are built for more ambitious goals which may take many years to achieve. BSCs are generally inspected every year. The annual review allows for bigger goals.

Can they be used together?

While both of these strategic frameworks are useful in their own right, they work best when used harmoniously. A strategy model called 'Two Speed Execution' has been developed that combines the strategy map of a BSC with the intricate objective definition of OKRs. BSCs are effective in creating long term goals for companies, while OKRs are great at breaking them down into smaller, more quantifiable results.

A Balanced Scorecard can be created as a way to initially outline strategy and major goals. Admins can then organize an OKR with the help of the information provided in BSCs. This has a more holistic approach to project management.

For instance, in a company when stakeholders and other higher authorities come together, they can collectively form the main organizational goals using BSCs, and use OKRs to set quarterly goals.

OKRs vs Balanced Scorecard- which one will you choose?

Both BSC and OKRs are tools used to manage performance and track progress, but companies tend to use them to address different issues in different scenarios. While it is believed that BSCs are suitable for annual or three-year target achievements, OKRs work best for shorter-term plans such as monthly or quarterly goals. OKRs are a newer form of progress evaluation, but they are not structured to replace BSCs. You will benefit the most by using the two frameworks in unison.

Check out this detailed comparison between balanced scorecard and OKRs to find out which framework works best for your goals:

Perspective	Balanced Scorecard	OKR
Methodology	Most companies will draft objectives and measurements that are designed to stay in place for at least one year or more. When constructing a Balanced Scorecard, organizations create objectives and measures in four distinct, yet related perspectives of performance: Financial, Customer, Internal Processes, and Learning & Growth	Most organizations change their Objectives and Key Results each quarter, focusing on what can create the most value in the next 90 days. OKRs do not have predefined categories. Individuals, teams, departments, and organizations decide what is most important in the next 90 days and align the organization from the bottom-up or top-down.
Advantage	Closely related to other aspects of performance and business, namely: · Strategy Maps · Risk Budgeting · Other business functions	· Companies use OKRs to structure the organization as a whole · Helps bridge the gap between strategy and execution · Helps teams identify issues from quarter to quarter so they can adjust and adapt
Process	BSC is usually an entirely top-down process; the leadership goes off and designs top-level goals that are then cascaded down throughout the organization. This means employees are focusing on the most important thing for the organization.	OKR is done bottom-up, sideways, as well as top-down. With OKRs, people have more freedom to design their own goals, or at least have more input into the process, which means they are more engaged with the objectives. It's also a more transparent process, because OKRs are visible across the entire company.
Implementation	BSC is often linked to compensation and bonuses, even if it's only partially linked (such as financial indicators that inform bonuses).	OKRs are completely separated from compensation discussions to prevent employees from "sandbagging" — or, setting a low target they know they will achieve. This encourages employees to set stretch goals.
Focus	Management	Management & Operations

How does the OKR framework compare to the Balanced Scorecard?

Conclusion

As many business leaders will tell you, a grand strategy is nothing without a strong foundation and the right resources for a project. Properly preparing to launch your OKR program is a vital step for any business looking to achieve their goals with this strategy-execution framework.

The key components of a successful OKR program have a lot to do with the business culture, the willingness of the team to learn from their mistakes, and the commitment to setting stretch targets and ambitious goals. This book has provided the foundational materials for you to prepare your business for OKRs. Before launching your OKR program, you need to define your success criteria, get a company-wide commitment to iterative business practices, and learn how OKRs fit into your daily processes. Decide how you want to monitor OKR progress throughout the quarter, and who will be involved in the planning process at the beginning of the quarter.

Once you've completed this preparation work, it's time to launch your OKR program. For expert advice on how to launch and manage your OKR program, look for *Launching Your OKR Program*, the next installment in this series.